Clc

Sis Ella Jackson

COPYRIGHT

Inspired by God

Author...Sis Ella Jackson

Adapted for publication...Omar S. Brooks

Editor...Christie Johnson

Photographer...W.B. Photography

Spiritual Consultants...Sis Ella Jackson...Minister Patty Reese

Promotions...Enertia Global, LLC

e-nertia global systems

Jesus had no Servants,
Yet they called him Master.

He had no Degree,
Yet they called him Teacher.

He had no Medicine,
Yet they called him Healer.

He had no Army,
Yet kings feared Him.

He won no military Battles,
Yet he Conquered the World.

He committed no Crime,
Yet they Crucified Him.

He was Buried in a tomb,
Yet he Rose in three days
And Lives Today!

He's the Same Yesterday,
Today, and Forever.

Amen

DEAR FAMILY

Dear Family and Friends,

Our country needs our prayers. Please pray for all the families that lost their loved ones in all the storms and hurricanes this year. Please pray for the sick and shut in. Someone prayed for you, so please, with your heart, keep them lifted up. May God give our President the wisdom and knowledge he needs to run this country, with courage, strength, and compelling commitment, so that when adversities arise, he stands firm knowing, that God is with him. Let him know that the battle belongs to God. Please keep President Barack Obama and his family lifted up in prayer. They need our prayers like we need the prayers of others.

I'm giving thanks to Almighty God for the gift of my mother, Monica Heisser, for bringing me in to this world and loving and caring for me the best she could. No one is perfect. My brother, Denton Heisser, and sister, Khadijah Miller, may God bless you and cover you all the days of your lives. To all my aunts, uncles, cousins (especially my favorite cousin, Ronald D. Brackett, for his faithfulness and trust and belief in me, I love you

4

deeply. Keep your head up.), and the White Family (most of all Mr. Robert LeGene Edward White Sr., the father of my oldest children, for giving me two beautiful children that have been a huge part of my life. I cannot ask God for anything else in this world. Thank you Robert), I love you all dearly. I thank God for all of you being a part of my life even for those that despised me. For my unknown father, I pray one day we meet before it is too late. Yes, I have for-given you for all the years that you haven't been in my life.

I'm also giving special thanks, love, and respect to my great aunt Geralene Chappell for all of her love for me and opening her doors when many were closed on me. Never-the-less, my most beloved, beautiful, late grandmother, Ella Mae Washington, a woman who never gave up even through her struggles,

trials and tribulations. Momma, I love you and miss you so dearly. I would also like to dedicate my first book to her. You told me if I put my mind to it, I can do anything. What a blessing having you in my life.
[Sept 5, 1937 – Dec 17, 2005]
In Jesus Name Amen!

ACKNOWLEDGEMENTS

First and foremost I want to thank Jehovah God for everything, mostly for life. I shouldn't be here, but he kept me in spite of my unfaithfulness, lies, deceit, and manipulations. I thank God for his Love for me, his Grace and Mercy ,that saved a wretch like me. In spite of my past, He never left me or gave up on me, when man did. God dusted me off and told me to start over. When people, and my relatives, judged me, God told me to pray for them and turn the other cheek. OH BOY! That was hard for me, but as time went on it became much easier. They saw the worst in me while God saw the best in me. I thank God for the love of my five gifted children that he blessed me with, Zechariah White, Robert White, Elohim Jackson, Adonia Jackson and Aqaveon Jackson, still have for me.

I once served the devil through my lack of faith and short-comings. Now, I serve God and my faith is renewed, my strength has multiplied. Oh God, thank you! I give you all the Glory and Praise.

I thank God for my husband, Johnny Jackson, who has been there through thick and thin. God bless his soul and may God continue to bless him.

I thank God for the foundation He set under my feet. He gave me my salvation and calling through Friendship Missionary Baptist Church in Columbus, Ohio. I want to thank you, Bishop and Mother Turner, for all your love, guidance, and support.

He gave me the Washington City Mission. He delivered me from crack-cocaine and alcohol. (I don't ever have to use if I don't put it in my hand.) (ONE DAY @ A TIME.) Just want to say thank you to the Pyramid Recovery Center for allowing me to come in and begin a second chance at life, and to all the techs, Landa, Essie, Lyle, Mike and OH BOY, my therapist Brad (what would I have done without all you guys and many more caring souls like yourselves!). God bless you all. My support group and (WE) The Care Center; Andy S. Bethany, Becky, Pat J., Andrew J. Kelly, Sally, and many more. Oh my God, you saved my life! I will forever love you all from the bottom of my gut. I pray that God will multiply your households and children. Last but not least, NA, a program that was so freely given to me. A God given program that taught me to be honest, open-minded, and have the willingness to do what ever it takes to stay clean. Don't take the 1st one, get a sponsor, a home group, get in service, work the 12 steps, 12 traditions, and the 12 concepts which is the program. This program only offers freedom from Active Addiction and a new way of life without the use of a chemical or a drug. Remember alcohol is a drug. I also thank AA for The Reprint for NA. You people mean a lot to me.

I want to give a special shout out to a very special lady God put in my life. We haven't had a lot of time together, but she knows God has me covered and if I need her or I'm in trouble I call ASAP. With all due respect, she is a God given mentor, a gifted woman, an anointed woman, a blessed and highly favored woman my sponsor, Johnnie Wallace. Love you sis, *Miss Dynamite*!

When you say you're grateful, remember that's an action word. So my blessed brother, Omar I truly thank God for the gift He has stirred up in you. I will always love you and thank you for taking time out for me to heal and help others heal.

To those who have hurt me in my process, I have forgiven you all, but you need to know ya'll kept me moving, motivated, trudging, laughing, praying more steadfast, and having the willingness to do what-ever I had to do to stay clean. Thank you all. I love you all and I'm going to continue to pray for you all to receive because you all deserve a chance to recover. Be blessed and be a blessing! -Sis Jackson

Introduction

This project has transformed my life. I entered into this deal as a publisher, putting aside my own publishing dreams to start a journey that has changed the scope of my beliefs. Honestly, I expected not much more than average ambition displayed across several note books, before I had seen first-hand the work Ella was creating, like magic, in her writing room. You see, I had been lost myself at the time this project began and forgot the changing power of God. I met the author months prior in a line at a discount store where I had never spoke to or seen her before. Something in my spirit told me to go up to her, introduce myself, and tell her things I still can't believe I said till this day. Only God can make the unfamiliar, familiar. You see, I told someone I'd never seen before nor ever met, that she was a writer and I was going to help her publish her book. To this day when we laugh about the power God had over our meeting at a chance encounter, I am amazed at what transpired. A few months later, there I was, sitting across from such an inspirational person, amazed by her energy and belief in not only herself but our God.

That's when it hit me, like lightening, strength, enough to brighten my life. I believed again for the first time in years. Here's why. I sat there in the kitchen looking through piles of notebooks and thought to myself this woman has been busy. She told me she cannot stop writing as if the Lord has touched her soul and pointed it in the direction of publication and helping others through her own experiences. I listened that night, inspired by her personal story and left with an ear full of understanding of why this first project was so important to her. I got right to work pushing my other projects aside and was captivated by what I began to read and though I didn't fully understand what was happening to me at that point in time, now I grasp the entire message and meeting behind that thirty second conversation at the store. God works in mysterious ways. That I understand. But, when He told me to only charge a dollar for the service, I asked myself if that was crazy. Even after many pain staking nights, I do not regret saying that over soft music in her kitchen as we hashed out the initial outline. I wanted only a dollar to symbolize the place the journey started at. I wanted a dollar because the physical no longer means as much to me as it once did. I wanted a dollar rather than anything else because I can frame it and keep it forever while all other monies would just end up in the wrong place. You see, the soul gets paid so much more than the body. I became richer upon the completion of this project. It inspired me to dust off my own faith and start on my own recovery toward a brighter future for myself with God as the number one source in my life from recovery till I part ways with this earth.

Here's what you'll take spiritually from this book; everyone has a recovery in the making. Everyone has something to recover from. Everyone can use a lesson from some part in this book. Recovery starts and is maintained one step at a time, day to day, one faithful inch at a time.

This project has set a foundation under my feet. I now stand firmer than ever before and offer this advice on how to read this book;

1. Use your bible in correlation with this book. There are areas of which involve reading biblical scriptures for further understanding of the message printed in those sections of the book. If you do not own a bible you can obtain one free of charge, in most circumstances, or purchase one relatively inexpensively. Reading the Bible helps with the recovery process and also solidifies the devotions offered.

2. This book was written for all reading age groups and made simple to follow because adversity knows no age limit. So, it was formatted with that principle in mind.

3. Seek guidance from a spiritual advisor and surround yourself with positive people during this process. This is the key when trying to step out against old worldly ways. If you keep negative people in your life, then negative will always find its way back into your life.

4. This book was not just written for Christians. Readers from all backgrounds and faiths can get something positive from taking on the journey of recovery. The core principles of this book can be applied to any situation to help anyone or any group recover from any situation in their lives. The strength of the Word is that powerful. Read a section at a time and understand what the devotion is trying to convey at that stage in your journey. You are as strong as the steps you take to get the most from this book.

5. Above all – never stop fighting against the evil that exists to break and take your soul. The journey you are about to take will be full of hurdles from outside influences, but remember turn one page of your life at a time and close all wounds.

This project has been a great blessing in my life. I know it will be a continual blessing and guide in yours. Seek ye the kingdom and watch the journey begin before your very eyes. This is it...your chance to gain ever-lasting freedom from addiction, pain, and/or affliction. This is your day...your chance.

-Omar S. Brooks...Publisher

Closing All Wounds

Part 1

The Needle = Strength

"For whosoever shall call upon the name of the Lord shall be saved." (Romans 10:13)

The beginning of your salvation starts with gathering your strength and preparing for the road ahead. Seek God's wisdom through the Word. Call upon the Lord for His mighty help through these and or any process so that you may come out victorious on the other side.

Here is where you find strength.

"But seek first the kingdom of God and His righteousness, and all these things shall be added to you." (Matthew 6:33 NKJV)

Open your Bible and bookmark this page from now till the end of your recovery.

This is your beginning. Come back to this scripture if you ever need to start over. Come back to this first step for guidance on where to go from there. From this point on you will be waging war for the battle over your soul. This is your **Needle**, your instrument of spiritual mending. This is your chance to close all wounds.

"Elisha sent a messenger to him, saying, Go and wash in Jordan seven times, and your flesh shall be restored, and you shall be clean. But Naaman was angry." (2 Kings 5:10-11)

We are all wounded in one way or another. Whether, physically, emotionally, or psychologically, we have all fallen short of the Lord God Almighty. Seek first His kingdom and the journey can start in your life today.

This is your day. Read and remember that you are blessed. Even now your wounds are healing.

Pray that your personal journey for change can begin with the turn of this page. Pray and ask for understanding of the Word. Let God have His way with your life today.

Take a moment to look back on everything that brought you to this point. Look back on every trial and tribulation that almost broke you, every sadness you have ever felt, and/or every spiritual sickness you have ever encountered.

Now...Never look back again.

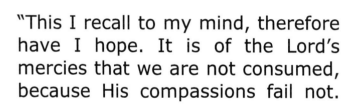

"This I recall to my mind, therefore have I hope. It is of the Lord's mercies that we are not consumed, because His compassions fail not.

They are new every morning: great is thy faithfulness."
(Lamentations 3:21-23)

Remember God is not your enemy. He's your protector, and healer of all wounds, mind, body and soul. **Seek him daily** and you'll find rest for the long journey.

God is full of compassion and understanding for the things going on in your life. He is faithful. This means He never fails you. You must remember this daily.

Remember that victory is yours. It has already been established.

Check to make sure your Bible is still bookmarked at:
Matthew 6:33 NKJV
Reread this scripture in a quiet place before continuing.

[Say these words with me.]
Dear Lord, Please help me to remember that you are my protector, helper, deliverer and

bridge over troubled waters. Thank You Father, In The Name Of Jesus Amen!

This day remember that you can find strength always in your provider. He can deliver you from any trial or tribulation. He is truly your salvation and a light at the end of agonizing darkness.

"Therefore do not worry and be anxious."
(Matthew 6:31)

The best remedy for those who are unhappy, lonely, or afraid is to take some breaths.

Say the **Serenity Prayer.**

God grant me the Serenity To except the things I cannot change. Courage to change the things I can and the Wisdom to know the difference.

Read Psalm 86
God knows your weaknesses. He will strengthen you.

Strength comes from a variety of places. Today let your strength come from your courage to move forward.

Do not worry or be anxious about the things you can not change alone. Write down the Serenity Prayer and post it in a visible place until the end of this book for added wisdom and strength.

God grant me the Serenity To except the things I cannot change. Courage to change the things I can and the Wisdom to know the difference.

[Book mark this page]

"Because he hath set his love upon me, therefore will I deliver him: I will set him on high, because he hath known my name. He shall call

23

upon me, and I will answer him: I will be with him in trouble; I will deliver him, and honor him." (Psalm 91:14-15)

When the strains of sin appear on your heart; God's cleansing power is much greater than Tide to go, we have grace and mercy to go.

Read Psalm 103

Remember being young and wanting something that you knew you couldn't have? Your salvation is not this way. You can claim your prize in glory and everlasting love through strengthening your commitment to follow Jesus and his teachings.

Remember it is never too late to begin this journey.
It is also never too late to rebuild your faith if you've back-slid spiritually.

Dust yourself off and get back up
"Therefore did my heart rejoice, and my tongue was glad; moreover also my fresh shall rest in hope: Because thou wilt not leave my soul in hell, neither wilt thou suffer thine Holy One to see corruption."

(Acts 2:26-27)

There's nothing too big, too small that God can't handle. Cast all your burdens on him for God cares for you. He will calm all your fears and storms. Remember, he is your strength and your bridge over troubled waters.

Sometimes, in life we are over-whelmed by the task ahead of us, over-whelmed by the bills piling up that need paid, or simply over-whelmed by the everyday stresses of life. Give your worry to Jesus. Let Him take on what may be troubling you, for nothing is too large an obstacle for God.

I've commanded you to be strong and brave. Don't ever be afraid or discouraged.
I am the Lord your God, I will be there to help you go. **I am there.**

God loves you.

Strength is the first step to closing all wounds simply because God has commanded you to be strong. He wants you to be brave in the face of doubt. He truly loves you more than you can imagine.

"The Lord said unto my Lord, Sit thou on my right hand, Until I make thy foes thy footstool." (Acts 2:34-35)

God will never take you through something without bringing you out on the winning side of grace. When you can't protect yourself **God will.**

" I exhort therefore, that, first of all, supplications, prayers, intercessions, and giving of thanks, be made for all men, For kings, and for all that are in authority; that we may lead a quiet and peaceable life in all Godliness and honesty." (Timothy 2:1-2)

There's no coincidence that you were saved or still here. God has a plan and a purpose for your life, and you need to stick and stay around long enough to find out what it is. **God is waiting for you. Stand up and be counted.**

"Remember your leaders and superiors in authority, [for it was they] who brought to you the Word of God. Observe attentively and consider their manner of living...and imitate their faith." (Hebrews 13-7)

Faith sees the future. It sees a future with charging and uncharted eyes of hope. Never give up! For, there is a God that hears all your prayers.

Follow the faithful and walk in their paths toward success.

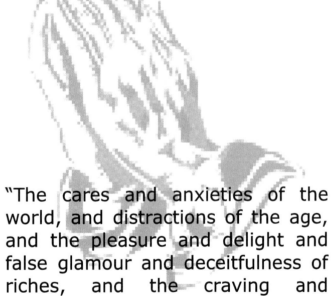

"The cares and anxieties of the world, and distractions of the age, and the pleasure and delight and false glamour and deceitfulness of riches, and the craving and passionate desire for other things creep in and choke and suffocate the Word, and it becomes fruitless." (Mark 4:19)

When you take care of your soul, all other areas of your life fall in line with God's plan for you. Your life will also have peace and understanding.

Manage your own spiritual maintenance and your strength will continue to grow.

"Love never fails"
(1 Corinthians 13:8)

Treat people like you want to be treated. They are human beings also. Treat them as a child of God. **God sees all,** so be loving, kind, and caring. Love God first, then yourself, and then you will be able to love others with a full and satisfied heart. Love like you've never been hurt.

Remember Jesus did not turn away from the way of love even when times were absolutely intolerable.

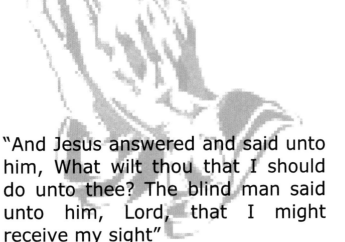

"And Jesus answered and said unto him, What wilt thou that I should do unto thee? The blind man said unto him, Lord, that I might receive my sight"
(From The Book of Matthew)

Take time to pray this morning, today might be one of those days that God has you on an assignment for someone else. Remember to walk in love and practice what you preach.

Pray about your wounds and how you want them to begin the process of closing. Let the Lord Jesus open your eyes and guide you in a direction where you will find the things you really need.

"For the grace of God that brings salvation has appeared to all men, teaching us that, denying ungodliness and worldly lusts, we should live soberly, righteously, and Godly in the present age, looking for the blessed hope and glorious appearing of our great God and Savior Jesus Christ, who gave Himself for us, that He might

redeem us from every lawless deed and purify for Himself His own special people, zealous for good works."
(Titus 2:11-14 NKJV)

Always keep God first.

Seek ye the kingdom of God first and all things shall be added unto you. If your priorities have been shifted I encourage you to get them back in line with the Master's plan.

Live how God wants you to live, righteously, soberly, and Godly.

This day remember these three things and think of a way to add them to your daily routine each and every-day.

"Be of good courage, And He shall strengthen your heart, All you who hope in the LORD." (Psalms 31:24 NKJV)

You don't have to settle for less today. God has all the riches you need in spirit.

He that lives in you is greater than he that is in the world.

Gifts come and go but salvation and a relationship with God will make you the head and not the tail.

Courage comes with standing up for what you believe in. It comes with saying I will not settle for less today. I will do right by my God and continue on my path to spiritual recovery.

"Restore us, O God; Cause your face to shine, and we shall **be saved**. Continue to allow God to change you into who you really are."
(Psalm 80:3)

This moment recall that God has the strength to heal your every wound. Remember to continue to pray and praise God. Remember he is your salvation and shelter in the time of storm.

"The wicked is banished in his wickedness, But the righteous has a refuge in his death." (Proverbs 14:32 NKJV)

Be aware of people, places, and things, you need to be watchful, **never let your guard down**. When your not guarded the enemy will sweep you like a flood and have you influenced by worldly things. Keep your eyes open and ears listening.

"He who believes in the Son has everlasting life; and he who does not believe in the Son shall not see life, but the wrath of God abides on him."
(John 3:36 NKJV)

Please don't give up on our Lord. God knows what's best for you and when to deliver you. Keep pressing on and don't let go of God's unchanging hand. God never changes, He's the same yesterday, today and forever.

Believe in the Son and begin your journey toward everlasting life. Be not of this world and it's possessions. Be an abider of His precious word.

"I have come as a light into the world, that whoever believes in Me should not abide in darkness." (John 12:46 NKJV)

God hears and sees all so don't ever stop praying just because you see no change. Keep pressing on. Pray until something happens.

"Faith without works is dead." James 2:20

God can take you out of any darkness through belief in him. If this day, you feel like there is darkness still in your heart, seek spiritual guidance before continuing to read on any further. Ask someone with experience reading the Word for help in better understanding the Lord's teachings. Ask the Lord for better understanding of His Word also. Continue to build your spiritual strength through belief and walking closer to God.

"The LORD is with you while you are with Him. If you seek Him, He will be found by you; but if you forsake Him, He will forsake you."
 (2 Chronicles 15:2 NKJV)

Therefore submit to God. Resist the devil and he will flee from you. Draw near to God and He will draw near to you.

"Cleanse your hands you sinners; and purify your hearts, you double- mined."

James 4:7-8

Remember that the Lord is with you while you are with Him. So, you are never alone as long as you keep Him in you heart.

"But without faith it is impossible to please Him, for he who comes to God must believe that He is, and that He is a rewarder of those who diligently seek Him." (Hebrews 11:6 NKJV)

Sometimes we have to let go of people in order for God to deal with them and work things out in their lives. **We can't live for others,** only for ourselves, but keep them in prayer.

"Blessed is the man who walks not in the counsel of the ungodly, Nor stands in the path of sinners, Nor sits in the seat of the scornful; But his delight is in the law of the LORD, And in His law he meditates day and night. He shall be like a tree planted by the rivers of water, That brings forth its fruit in its season, Whose leaf also shall not wither; And whatever he does shall prosper."
(Psalm 1:1-3 NKJV)

People come and go, words cut like a knife, and relationships are expired, but we still hold on, for fear of being alone, unwanted, and unloved. There is no greater love than the love of God. God is faithful when you're not, and a comforter.

"For the LORD loves justice, and does not forsake His saints; They are preserved forever, but the descendants of the wicked shall be cut off." (Psalm 37:28 NKJV)

What is love really? Do you really know? Well, I'll tell you! Love is kind and patient, never jealous, boastful, proud, nor rude. Love isn't selfish or quick tempered. It doesn't keep a record of wrongs others do. Love rejoices in the truth, but not in evil. Love is always supportive, loyal, hopeful, and trusting. **Love never fails**. (1 Corinthians 13:4-8)

"And my God shall supply all your need according to His riches in glory by Christ Jesus." (Philippians 4:19 NKJV)

You don't have to forget the past, but you have to **forgive yourself and others and move on**. Don't let the past hinder your future especially when it is bright and glorious with God on your side.

"For God so loved the world that He gave His only begotten Son, that whoever believes in Him should not perish but have everlasting life."
(John 3:16 NKJV)

Know that in spite of your circumstances, that if you stay in prayer and **don't give up**, God is faithful to bring you through. Only you can stop the pain and your blessings.

God showed his love for you. Now, show your love for God by being strong and never giving up on your journey toward a better tomorrow.

"Sow for yourselves righteousness; Reap in mercy; Break up your fallow ground, For it is time to seek the LORD, Till He comes and rains righteousness on you."
(Hosea 10:12 NKJV)

God will not take you through something without bringing you out.

Continue the hard work you are doing to recover your soul. Do not give up before the change can take place in your life

"Most assuredly, I say to you, he who believes in Me has everlasting life." (John 6:47 NKJV)

My dear friends, **stand firm** and don't be shaken. Always keep busy working for the Lord.
Know that your building a relationship that is priceless. You know that everything you do for him is worth while.

Read: 1 Corinthians 15:58

"Why are you cast down, O my soul? And why are you disquieted within me? Hope in God; For I shall yet praise Him, The help of my countenance and my God." (Psalms 42:11 NKJV)

The worst thing to do when your going through turbulent waters is to shut down and not reach out. Isolation is a trap set by the enemy. Reach out to someone and let them know what's really going on with you. Break the cycle of bondage. **Reach out**. Believe that there is more to be done in your life. God can use you today. You are stronger now than you were when you started this journey. Now, it's time to set a spiritual structure in your life that no man can topple.

Remember your strength can be intensified through your belief and hard work at establishing a belief that you are strong and ready for the task ahead. Believe in yourself and you will be ready for the next step in closing your wounds.

Notes:

Closing All Wounds

Part 2

The Thread =Foundation

Setting a strong foundation to anchor yourself to God and build a strong foundation for spiritual success.

"And Jesus said to them, "I am the bread of life. He who comes to Me shall never hunger, and he who believes in Me shall never thirst."
(John 6:35 NKJV)

Exercise: On a sheet of paper

- Write down three strong people in your life.

- Next to their names give two reasons they are strong.
- Circle any of these reasons that you would like to apply to your recovery.
- Keep this with you physically or mentally until you reach part three.

"Blessed be the God and Father of our Lord Jesus Christ, who according to His abundant mercy has begotten us again to a living hope through the resurrection of Jesus Christ from the dead"
(1 Peter 1:3 NKJV)

What a mighty God we serve that shows us unconditional love, grace, and unchanging friendship. Stay focused. **Always trust God,** not man. Start building a stronger spiritual foundation by surrounding yourself with the building blocks to successful renewal and focus. Simply put, surround yourself with spiritually sound persons, surround yourself with the light of God that will brighten your life, and start a routine to read the Word daily. Look for a spiritual mentor who can help you on your path to building a stronger foundation with the Lord.

"The LORD is good to those who wait for Him, to the soul who seeks Him."
(Lamentations 3:25 NKJV)

Trusting in the Lord will help you set a spiritual cornerstone in your life.
Don't trust anyone, not even your best friend, and be careful what you say to the one you love.

Read: Micah 7:5

"For You are my hope, O Lord GOD; You are my trust from my youth." (Psalms 71:5 NKJV)

God, you have been there for me time and time again during my many wrongs and backslidings. I have continued to fall short of you. I understand this now. Please show mercy for me and continue to bless me. Keep strength in my heart, my feet on solid ground and my soul ready for the action of praising your name and being a greater witness for you.

Let today be a joyous, pain free day for your next step in spiritual growth. Your spiritual debts have been cancelled, your pain from years of bad wounds removed. God has forgiven you. He will never remind you of the past, just the future. He loves you.

"To Him all the prophets witness that, through His name, whoever believes in Him will receive remission of sins." (Acts 10:43 NKJV)

Continue believing in yourself and the power that GOD possesses. He alone is your salvation. Believe in Him and remember that you are never alone when a test comes your way. Temptation tests your spirit. Do not let it ever shatter your foundation with GOD again. Believe that you will receive remission of your sins.

Just for today, have some gratitude. Give thanks to God for allowing you to go through some stuff and bring you all the way out

safely without falling to the wayside.
God Is Good!

"But as many as received Him, to them He gave the right to become children of God, to those who believe in His name: who were born, not of blood, nor of the will of the flesh, nor of the will of man, but of God."
(John 1:12-13 NKJV)

Seek and ask God for understanding of His word daily and remember that today is your day to reclaim your victory with Jesus.

It's really a time to take back all that the Devil has stolen from you. Wage war on the Enemy. Go in to this war without fear and come out with blessings.

"The hand of our God is upon all those for good who seek Him, but His power and His wrath are against all those who forsake Him." (Ezra 8:22 NKJV)

Grace is upon you. Do well in taking advantage of this time. Walk and talk with a new stride in your step and a new tone on your tongue because you are stronger today than you were yesterday. Continue to read the Word of God and follow the teachings of your spiritual mentor.

Praise God for another day! He didn't have to wake you, yet you're alive. Isn't He good? Now that you're up, it is time to do what he has called or asked you to do faithfully. Amen.

Dear Father,
Enable me to manage my time more effectively. For idle time is the Devil's worship time. Teach me to make time for You everyday and night being still, waiting on You. In Jesus' Name, Amen!

Men waste time dwelling on the things they cannot change. Give your time to the LORD and let all things filter through Him. He has the power to make the most of your time. Give Him your life and watch the good out way the bad. Sacrifice the unclean things you used to do with the clean practices you are now beginning.

"The God of all grace who called you to His everlasting glory in Christ, will restore, confirm, strengthen, and establish those who have suffered a little while."
(1 Peter 5:10)

Don't worry. God has you through it all.

You've been through so much this year. Do not let the devil win ever again. His work is continuously trying and testing you. Keep him outside your foundation by surrounding yourself with the Grace of the Lord. Surround yourself with more positive people. Let the Word of God guide you through any test in front of you. Because you know now that they are coming and are constant. Your only way ahead is to never go back down that old rocky, unclean road again. God has you through it all. God loves you through it all. God is good and gladness is just around the corner.

Be kindly affectionate to one another with brotherly love.

Read Romans 12:10

We all have flaws!!! It's never too late to be kind, but it is too late when that hour has come and gone.

You've heard the saying now live through the action of doing so. Treat people as you would like to be treated. Be compassion for God's creations. Think not of yourself but of God's will and keep love in your heart. Remember, we are all flawed and no man is perfect. You are better with Jesus than alone and in the dark. Seek the light always and never go back to that dreaded place you once were.

"For I know the thoughts that I think toward you, says the LORD, thoughts of peace and not of evil, to give you a future and a hope. Then you will call upon Me and go and pray to Me, and I will listen to you. And you will seek Me and find Me, when you search for Me with all your heart."
(Jeremiah 29:11-13 NKJV)

With all your heart you must trust the Lord and not your own judgment. Always let him lead you, and he will clear your road for you to follow. Don't ever think you are wise enough. Respect the Lord and stay away from evil.

Read Proverbs 3:5-7

Don't worry about tomorrow. Stay focused on today, for tomorrow will take care of itself. God is faithful to provide all you need. His Word is never void.

Read Matthew 6:25-34

Be blessed the word is your meal.

God shows us love every morning we wake up and we need to show others love daily. There are so many hurt people in the world that need to know they're loved.

God says;

"My grace is sufficient for fou, for My strength is made perfect in weakness."
2 Corinthians 12:9

Remember, part one talked about strength. That is because you will continue to build and develop your strength through your own personal and spiritual growth. It had to be your beginning. Let it not end there because in every step you take in life, you will need to reach and sometimes rediscover this source of energy against any and all threats to your soul. God's love and protection are sufficient for you to pass any test. When you fail its because you wanted that earthly thing more than God's love. The earthly things you used to use will never get you closer to being a stronger more successful man or woman of God. Let these things lay in the past where your old self is now and never look back, for it is awkward to walk forward while looking back.

I pray that you have a blessed day today in spite of what's going on keep serving and loving your self and others. Let God's will be done and not yours, and keep your mind on Him. God will keep you in perfect peace.

Read: Isaiah 26:3

What does this scripture mean to you?

Notes:

Be a doer and not a taker.
Be a giver and not a receiver.
Be a blessing and not a curse.
Be a prayer warrior and not a worrier.

Sometimes keeping it simple is the best way to get the point across. The above devotion simply means, be the success that God wants you to be.

Be not disturbed by your surroundings, or circumstances. God is in control and handling everything. Press on. There is hope and a light at the end of the darkest tunnel.

"By humility and the fear of the LORD are riches and honor and life."
(Proverbs 22:4 NKJV)

Fear is not always a bad thing. God's faithful followers fear losing His love and grace. This is a healthy fear because it keeps one wanting to do right by Him. Do right in your everyday situations with God's people and you'll find right comes back your way. You are blessed. You can read these words and are able to make a choice to act on them or turn the other way. Some are not so fortunate. Things can always be worse. Keep this in mind when going through tough times before God's blessing rains down upon you and remain faithful. Be not of this earth when the blessing is ready for you. Your riches are with the Lord and nothing else is worth the weight of his Glory and Honor.

If you're struggling and going through trying times today, you don't have to be by yourself. Turn it over to God. He'll work it out. God is the Master of turning burdens into blessings.

Ask God to strengthen your foundation. Pray that your feet stay on solid ground. From this point on, keep only positive people in your life.

Know that the past was to learn from and make you stronger. God has a purpose and a plan for your life. You live and you learn. Simply put but enough to build upon, after reading these lines think of three things you wish you could take back from your past. Write them down on a sheet of paper. Close your eyes and pray that they are forgiven. Ask for forgiveness. Ask for protection from ever going back on these old ways. Ask for continued guidance. Pray for others who may have the same affliction. Praise God for already working miracles in your life. Open your eyes. Fold the paper until you can no longer fold it any more. Now, throw it in the trash. You are forgiven. Keep your mind on the

Lord and never look back on those things again.

Read The Book of Matthew and do not move on until you have read it completely.

Ask God for understanding of His Word.

Notes:

Welcome back to the rest of a better life for yourself. You feel better today than you have in sometime. Your wounds are starting to heal. Yet, you understand there is so much farther to go. Seek guidance from your spiritual mentor about any questions you may have from reading The Book of Matthew and remember that progress is being made, a soul is being saved, and a body and it's wounds are mending.

Look beyond your hurt and flaws. Stay out of harms way by walking in the light of the Lord. God has forgiven you of all your sins. God loves you more than you can imagine. Today look over your life and see how God has kept you in all your difficulties.

"Not that I speak in regard to need, for I have learned in whatever state I am, to be content: I know how to be abased, and I know how to abound. Everywhere and in all things I have learned both to be full and to be hungry, both to abound and to suffer need. I can do all things through Christ who strengthens me."
(Philippians 4:11-13 NKJV)

God's word encourages us to strive for maturity and integrity daily. Have you done an inventory lately?

Take a minute to write down five things/people that make you feel strong, happy, or successful. Keep these things with you till the end of this book.

God gives us strength for tomorrow's pain.

"Now faith is the substance of things hoped for, the evidence of things not seen."
(Hebrews 11:1 NKJV)

Have you hoped for things to get better but it seems as though there is no end to your anguish? There is an end in sight. Everything that begins must end. That means every time you're going through the worst the world can throw at you, there is an end in sight. You must remain faithful through these times. You must keep your mind on Jesus and his teachings. Never let these times get the best of you ever again. The evidence that God is good will come in the form of the event passing, your pain being lifted away, and/or a lightening of the heavy load you may feel you have to bear alone. You are never alone. Faith will carry you through. You will become stronger in the end.

Be diligent in everything you do. Honor the Lord at all times. Love, live, and laugh like there's no tomorrow. Your spiritual foundation is now strong. Believe in its strength. Understand, however, that there is so much farther to go. Keep with a support group that brings you closer to God. Keep setting positive and obtainable goals. Try to read the entire bible, one important word at a time. You are strong today whether you believe it or not, and ready for the next step in your ever-changing spiritual renewal.

Read the book of Luke before continuing on. Ask yourself these questions;

- What can I learn from this book?

- What lessons can I apply to my everyday situations from these lessons?

- What don't I understand about this book?

- Who is the right person to answer these questions?

- What book follows Luke in the Bible?

- How can I start a routine to read all the books of the Bible?

(Seek guidance before continuing to read on to Part 3 with any or all unanswered questions you may have.)

Closing All Wounds

Part 3

The Procedure =Action

Action develops change. Continual work in any relationship will help secure its success. Take action in your life by following the routine you set up for yourself, by being faithful, and by exercising patience in the belief that you are changing for the better, each day, every day you read the Word of God.

Besides, if you've made it this far you're already making progress. This section will deal with managing yourself while starting to do God's work and understanding more of what he wants from you. The Procedure is Action in the face of difference, it means going against the flow of the old things you used to do and plotting your own course for those to follow your shining example. The Procedure is another step in Closing All Wounds and making your way to spiritual freedom from sin.

"Wherefore I put thee in remembrance that thou stir up the gift of God...Who hath saved us, and called us with a holy calling, not according to our works, but according to his own purpose and grace, which was given us in Christ Jesus before the world began."
(2 Timothy 1:6, 9)

I asked myself once, if I was doing what I was meant to be doing. So, now I ask you the same. Are you doing what God intended for you to be doing? Some of us have asked this question, and yes it is an old one, but still there are a few that haven't. No matter how you answer the question, the truth is that God has put a calling in each of us. What is your calling? Pray God reveals it to you if He already has not. Pray for an action plan to complete the steps necessary to fulfill His plan for you.

"With long life will I satisfy [you], and show [you] my salvation." (Psalm 91:16)

God has made you the way He wants you to be, not the way man says, so accept who you are. You are the seed. God is the rain that will help you reach toward achieving anything you set out to accomplish through His wisdom, power, and grace. So, this day your action word is POWER. Be powerful in your pursuit of a better tomorrow.

"The Joy of the Lord is your strength"
(Nehemiah 8:10)

Keep your priorities in order, God, self, and family. If your priorities get somehow shifted or out of order and God isn't first, the rest will destroy you quickly. Keep God first. He is head of the body. Just follow His Powerful lead.

"He who guards his mouth and his tongue keeps himself from troubles."
(Proverbs 21:23
The Amplified Bible)

Let your words be in line with God's. Let your words be acceptable to God. Keep this in mind from day to day. Keep your temper under wraps, if this is an area where your tongue can be a bit more un-worry of God's love. Often a sinner's belief does not last as long as it should, because the sinner starts off with good intensions, but doesn't wait for the fruits of his labor to ripen. Be more patient this year. Let all fool language go to the wayside and practice great communication with the Lord through prayer (and yes, conversation) with your creature.

You can't sit around with idle time because the devil will sneak up on you. Then he has you. Especially people, places, and things...if you don't know them, leave them alone.

"And be not comforted to this world: but be ye transformed by the renewing of your mind."
(Romans 21:23
The Amplified Bible)

Let the God of your understanding guide, lead, and direct you today through whatever it is going on in your life. When the storm comes, don't run, dance in it. Your victory is near.

"For where envy and strife is, there is confusion and every evil work." (James 3:16)

Take control of your life and your household by setting the example to be followed. There may be others hurting that do not know the way to their salvation, but you can be an example of how change is evident and true. Stay on your plan to read all the books of the Bible. Keep continual contact with your spiritual advisor. If you still do not have one, seek out a positive person to help motivate you and keep you energized about the Lord. Most of all, at this point keep order in your life.

God is a God of Law and Order; if you haven't got your life and house in order then I suggest you start to do this today. Lean not on your own understanding, but on every Word of God.

"Jesus is the same yesterday, today, and forever."
(Hebrews 13:8)

The roots of stability come from being grounded in God's word with prayer. I dare you throughout this year to seek God, pray, and watch Him do miracles in your life and restore any brokenness.

"Endure hardness, as a good soldier of Jesus Christ."
(2 Timothy 2:3)

We must keep our houses in order. Stand on a solid foundation while letting no-one destroy it.
We show our love for God when we follow His plans for us to become stronger foundations in Christ. We show our love for God when we praise His name, read, and love His people.

"And be clothed with humility: for God resisteth the proud, and giveth grace to the humble."
(1 Peter 5:5)

Stop fighting to believe you are the righteousness of God. You've seen and read the Word of God and still want to believe your own thoughts and beliefs. Be a follower of good faith. Stay focused and humble. True humility is just that, staying humble to your vow to take action in your life.

Don't let your spirit be cluttered. Keep your thoughts clean by focusing on the Word of God. Take some time to clean up the junk and/or mess that's accumulated over time. Keep in prayer. One day at a time your situation will get better if you believe, make the effort, and trust in the Word.

"And these signs shall follow them that believe...they shall lay hands on the sick, and they shall recover."
(Mark 16:17-18)

You must feel to heal. Imagine you're holding your hand over a lit match. The heat from the flame will burn you if you let it. The sensation tells your nerves to tell your brain to move your hand away from the flame. You must trust in the change about to happen and feel the change as it is occurring. That feeling will help you through your trials and tribulations that may still be on the horizon ahead of you. That feeling is God awakening you, healing you, saving you. Act on this feeling. Testify. Give thanks to the Lord.

You are so close to recovery. Read the scripture above again for more self-worth and clarification.

"Study to show thyself approved unto God, a workman that needeth not to be ashamed."
(2 Timothy 2:15)

Do we ever get tired of our jobs? The answer for most of us is yes, yet household business must be taken care of also. Most of us don't want to work because of exhaustion. Tired of being tired? Then, work for God, his retirement plan is out of this world!

"Let the word of Christ dwell in you richly…"
(Colossians 3:16)

Satan offers nothing but tricks, deceit, and lies. What he couldn't accomplish last year, he will work overtime on this year. The Devil does not have new tricks, just new faces. Let God's Word dwell in you, so when evil tries to make you fall it knows your soul is good and with God.

The Devil is deceitful. You Better Watch!

Consider this:
you relapse before you pick up the drug because it's a process. It's a thinking process. Then it becomes physical. Once it becomes physical…it's over. You will use and you will lose. No if, ands, or buts.

"If any of you lacks wisdom, let him ask of God, who gives to all liberally and without reproach, and it will be given to him. But let him ask in faith, with no doubting, for he who doubts is like a wave of the sea driven and tossed by the wind."
(James 1:5-6 NKJV)

It is written, man shall not live by bread alone but by every word of God.

Read Luke 4:4.

The way to escape temptation is to focus on God.

"So too the (Holy) Spirit comes to our aid and bears us up in our weakness; for we do not know what prayer to offer...but the Spirit Himself ...pleads on our behalf with unspeakable yearnings and groanings too deep for utterance."
(Romans 8:26
The Amplified Bible)

Don't ever claim lifeless things or what you don't have. God knows your struggles, and/or confusion. We always have more then enough when God is our supplier. Let your Spirit guide your life not your body or mind. Your body is weak and is subject to death, but your spirit can endure forever.

"I will give unto thee the keys of the kingdom of heaven: and whatsoever thou shalt bind on earth shall be bound in heaven: and whatsoever thou shalt loose on earth shall be loosed in heaven." (Mathew 16:19)

I know not by what methods are; the Lord provides for us, I only know that all our needs He meets so graciously. What God promises he will provide.

"Nay in all these things we are more than conquerors through him that loves us."
(Romans 8:37)

God's not into giving you thrills. So, when he shows up (in some powerful dramatic mountain top way,) it is so that you would be some one different. He's not out to impress you. He wants to change you.

Read Ephesians 12.

"I wrote you in my previous letter not to associate(closely and habitually) with unchaste (impure) people."
(1 Corinthians 5:9)

Let's stop condemning each other. Decide instead to live in such a way that you will not cause another believer to stumble or fall. Surround yourself with positive people who will help you continue to build on your strong foundation.

"And we were in our own sight as grasshoppers, and so we were in their sight."
(Numbers 13:33)

A friend loves at all times, but in order to be a friend, you have to be a friend to yourself. Let us be to others what we desire for ourselves.

Read Proverbs 18:24

"The beginning of strife is as when water first trickles [from a crack in a dam]; therefore stop contention before it becomes worse and quarreling breaks out."
(Proverbs 17:14)

Be prepared to do something you've never done in order to go places you've never been. The road traveled by you is not always smooth and problem free. You are faced with rocky, broken roads at different points in your life. Yet, through God's strength you can navigate any obstacle that gets in the way of your true happiness.

"Whosoever heareth these sayings of mine, and doeth them I will liken him unto a wise man, which built his house upon a rock."
(Matthew 7:24)

We were built to serve God. We were created to praise His name and outlast the world. Seek God's everlasting wisdom in all you do. Serve God as He wants you to serve Him. Read His word and continually build own your own individual wisdom. Believe in the Power of His precious love for you.

"If any of you lack wisdom, let him of God, that giveth to all men liberally, and upbraideth not; and shall be given him." (James 1:5)

If you are going through turbulent waters don't blame God. Blame your self. Sometimes you need to get out of your own way and let God work it out for you. God is the answer not you. You can't win without God. He can settle the most devastating storm, calm your most trying tribulations, and set your feet on solid ground.

Give honor to God.

"This cup is the new covenant [ratified and established] in My blood."
(1 Corinthians 11:25)

Isn't it good to know yourself on the other side of life, for God has truly blessed you, and you don't see it. Look at your reflection. Whisper the words "God is good," and smile for He is a just and patient God. He is a way through all imperfections, impurities, and unholy worldly ways. See the person God created you to be and seek to be that strong minded student of the Word each day. Praise God.

Seek the confidence that Abraham had. Become a faith giant. Read the Word daily and ask for understanding.

"Now unto him that is able to do exceeding abundantly above all that we ask or think, according to the power that worketh in us."
(Ephesians 3:20)

God has been there. He has been your protector in the dark alleys, a shield from the worst the world can throw at you, a shelter in the time of storm. Nothing is too great for God. There is great hope in your future because He will be there guiding you over unsteady obstacles just as He was yesterday and the days passed the scope of memory.

Take one day at a time.

"For the Lord seeth not as man seeth; for man looketh on the outward appearance, but the Lord looketh on the heart."
(1 Samuel 16:7)

Let go of people, places and things that are not of God. Surround your-self with only things that will lift you higher and closer to God. Let go of all else for these are not worth your time, as it is precious. Spend your time as God intended and has commanded. Keep Him in your heart.

"God hath raised us up together, and made us sit together in heavenly places in Christ Jesus: That in the ages to come he might show the exceeding riches of His grace in His kindness toward us through Christ Jesus."
(Ephesians 2:6-7)

Your happiness is inside you. Allow no man to take that inner light away from you. Seek more elements found in the Word to make your inner light brighter. Allow your Spirit to awaken. Allow your happiness to let you be contagious. Share the joy of knowing God with the world and you will know gladness.

Your better today than you were yesterday!

"For we walk by faith, not by sight."
(2 Corinthians 5:7 NKJV)

Love yourself today because God loves you everyday. God loves you whether you know it or not, whether you see it or not. God's love is the greatest unconditional kind of love. You can't write or find the words to express His true love for you. Love yourself today. Love yourself tomorrow and every day there-after. Never again let hate take up the space in your heart that God is looking to fill. God's love will leave you feeling full and at times, satisfied beyond belief.

"So Jesus answered and said to them, "Have faith in God. For assuredly, I say to you, whoever says to this mountain, 'Be removed and be cast into the sea,' and does not doubt in his heart, but believes that those things he says will be done, he will have whatever he says." (Mark 11:22-23 NKJV)

Don't put your trust in people. People will fail you as they are not perfect. Put all your trust in God. He cannot lie or fail. **Trust God** and you'll find Peace and Understanding.

"But without faith it is impossible to please Him, for he who comes to God must believe that He is, and that He is a rewarder of those who diligently seek Him." (Hebrews 11:6 NKJV)

Let today be a joyful day. Thank God for what you have. Bless him for what you don't have. Life is a treasure and a precious ruby.

Live, love, and laugh today.

"...them that honor me I honor, and they that despite me shall be lightly esteemed."
(1 Samuels 2:30)

Be true to your own self. Start to love yourself and see yourself for who you really are. You are worthy to be alive. If it wasn't so, you would not be here. Learn to encourage yourself daily. Tell yourself you are blessed and highly favored. Pray for wisdom.

"The redeemed of the Lord shall return, and come with singing unto Zion; and everlasting joy shall be upon their head: they shall obtain gladness and joy; and sorrow and [grief] shall flee away."
(Isaiah 51:11)

If looking back hurts you and looking forward scares you, then look at today and do your best to change for the good. God will help you overcome all obstacles in your path clearing a way for a brighter more promising future. Pray for guidance.

"For by grace you have been saved through faith, and that not of yourselves; it is the gift of God, not of works, lest anyone should boast."
(Ephesians 2:8-9 NKJV)

Ever been tired of being tired? Face it. We all have felt this way at one point in time or another, yet whether you're feeling lonely, hurt, or wounded, God knows what to do to bring a lasting peace into your life. Be still and wait on God. He knows what is best for you. Pray for Peace in your life. Pray for a calming of the storm. Seek God.

I pray for your mind to be renewed, your heart to be cleansed, and your spirit to be awakened this day.

Let God move things in to place so that you are better off in a close but unseen tomorrow so that your heart is pure and full of peace and joy. In Jesus' Name Amen.

Exercise: On a sheet of paper

- Write down three things you want to improve in your life.
- Next to these things right down how you will start to improve on these areas.

Compare these findings with the previous exercise to analyze and build on your strength, foundation, and action toward a closer recovery.

"I call heaven and earth to record this day against you, that I have set before you life and death, blessing and cursing; therefore choose life, that both thou and thy seed may live."
(Deuteronomy 30:19)

Always speak joy, happiness, and good-will over a person or situation. Let the words of your mouth be acceptable by God in encouraging your own spiritual growth as well as others.

Life and death are in the power of the tongue.

Read James 3.

"But continue thou in the things which thou hast learned and hast been assured of, knowing of whom thou hast learned them."
(2 Timothy 3:14)

I heard someone say the Word of God is older than Creation but newer and more accurate than tomorrow's newspaper. News articles may come and go but the Word of God stands firm. Different topics may flood the news from time to time only to fade as viewers become less interested, but **the Word of God stands firm**. Inventions may change the way we read or listen to the ever-changing music of our generations that often ruin minds, mislead youth, and misdirect saved souls, yet the Word of God stands firm. Follow your heart. Follow the Word.

Closing All Wounds

Part 4

Recovery = Freedom

Recovery means that you are free from all that has kept you bound. You have overcome the world. Your chains have been broken. It has always been God's will that you chose Him.

Recovery means to get back. This is the part of your process where you take back your life. The second definition means to regain health. Enough said. If you don't use, your body can reform along with your mind, and Spirit. Reform means to improve. You cannot improve continuing unjust and/or unclean things. The second definition of reform is to abolish abuses. Need I say more? This is so important. Can't you see the light at the end of the tunnel? You're so close. Keep on your path to success. The Lord will guide you the rest of the way.

"Except the Lord build the house, they labour in vain that built it." (Psalm 127:1)

Keep on your road to a successful recovery in the spiritual essence of your soul. Meaning; walk in faith through good and bad times. Keep focused on the Lord even when the boat gets rocky. Know that He can calm any storm. Take time to heal. Take time to reflect on all God has done in your life and give thanks unto the Lord. Recovery isn't always easy. Anything worth while usually isn't. Calm your thoughts and set your mind on Jesus. Ask him to help you through all times of uneasiness, present and future.

"So shall my word be that goeth forth out of my mouth: if shall not return unto me void, but it shall accomplish that which I please, and it shall prosper in the thing whereto I sent it."
(Isaiah 55"11)

God made you an original, so don't let the world make you a counterfeit or a copy. Be all that you can be in his glorious light and obey God at all times. Your rewards are in heaven not earth. Do not get led by falsities and claims for a quick connection with the Lord God Almighty. Your rewards are in heaven, not anything of this earth.

Hold on...it will all get better.

"Humble yourself therefore under the mighty hand of God, that he may exalt you in due time: Casting all your care upon him; for he careth for you."
(1 Peter 5:6)

Today I ask God that we still pray for our country, our neighbors in need of prayer and those that are taking a closer walk with God. All the soldiers that fight for us daily are in my prayers this day. This is a new year, may they be blessed, protected, and covered by the Blood of Jesus. Amen.

Stay humble and everything will work itself out in your life.

"Not by might, nor by power, but by my sight, saith the Lord of hosts."
(Zechariah 4:6)

Give yourself a break by being still. Waiting on God will bring you much reward. You deserve a break. You've been struggling with something you can't undo on your own. Never give up. Exercise Patience by waiting for the blessing to fully transpire. Patience is a virtue.

"Give to others, and God will give to you. Indeed, you will receive a full measure, a generous helping, poured into your hands-all that you can hold. The measure you use for others is the one that God will use for you."
(Luke 6:38)

When you think of things in your life as detours they might just be those roads of destiny that are needed for your future. God has a plan for you.

Give and receive God's plan for your life.

"And these words, which I command thee this day shall be in thine heart: And thou shalt...talk of them when thou sittest in thine house, and when thou walkest by the way, and when thou liest down, and when thou risest up...and they shall be as frontlets between thine eyes."
(Deuteronomy 6:6-8)

So many stop before the Miracle happens. Make the first step. Be Still. Start your new life today. Be Still. Receive God's blessing for you. Be Still. Give praise to God, open up your heart for His teachings, let your light shine bright for all to see and Be Still. Be Still, Be Still, and Be Still!

You are worthy of all God has in store for you.

"He who trusts in his riches will fall, But the righteous will flourish like foliage."
(Proverbs 11:28 NKJV)

You can't base your life or your recovery on yesterday's plans but only for today. For it is a new day. If you messed up today you can always start your day over.

God will forgive you when people won't.

"The LORD is gracious and full of compassion, slow to anger and great in mercy."
(Psalms 145:8 NKJV)

Don't let go of God's unchanging hand. Letting go means being lost forever. Keep God first and the rest will fall in place.

Have you ever been in a situation where everything fell right into place?

Have you ever been in a situation that you never thought you'd get out of, and yet you did?

These are just a few examples of God's favor. God will put who he wants in your life to help you in your process.

Trust no-one but God and Love everyone.

"For the LORD God is a sun and shield; The LORD will give grace and glory; No good thing will He withhold from those who walk uprightly."
(Psalms 84:11 NKJV)

Allow God to take you to the restoration hardware store, it is not the most appealing store, but it's an advance place for you to regain what you need for your tool box. Have you looked in yours today?

"And let us not grow weary while doing good, for in due season we shall reap if we do not lose heart."
(Galatians 6:9 NKJV)

There's no way you can love someone if you don't love yourself. Practice loving yourself before others. This doesn't mean to be selfish. No, there is a way to exercise selfless service and still have esteem in your self. Seek God for strength through all things minor and major and let His light lead you to develop a greater sence of your own self worth.

"Let us hold fast the confession
of our hope without wavering,
for He who promised is faithful."
(Hebrews 10:23 NKJV)

I heard yesterday that we were
warriors, barriers, survivors, and
created to survive. The Devil Can't
Kill Who God Wants Alive. Keep
your heads up and know that you
are in good hands.

"For you have need of endurance, so that after you have done the will of God, you may receive the promise;" (Hebrews 10:36 NKJV)

We will always have trials and tribulations, but God will carry you through. Remember love is a battle. Every battle you win helps you to succeed and strive for more. Have faith in the process in which God has already written over your soul. Have faith and He will grant your every need.

"A good man obtains favor from the LORD, But a man of wicked intentions He will condemn." (Proverbs 12:2 NKJV)

No matter where you are, where you go, or who you're with, you always take your new blessed self with you. God knows all. There are no secrets. Remember that today you are in recovery and each day after this day you are in His grace.

Please pray first to make the right decisions from here on out and for understanding of His continued plan of growth for you. Everything will work itself out for the good.

"Therefore be patient, brethren, until the coming of the Lord. See how the farmer waits for the precious fruit of the earth, waiting patiently for it until it receives the early and latter rain. You also be patient. Establish your hearts, for the coming of the Lord is at hand." (James 5:7-8 NKJV)

Concentrate on this:
To get something you never had, you have to do somethings you've never done. When God takes something from you He's not punishing you. He's merely opening your hands to receive something better. The Will of God will never take you, where the Grace of God will not Protect you!

You are loved!

"My brethren, count it all joy when you fall into various trials, knowing that the testing of your faith produces patience. But let patience have its perfect work, that you may be perfect and complete, lacking nothing."
(James 1:2-4 NKJV)

Have you checked yourself lately? Is your fruit of the Spirit: Love, peace, joy, longsuffering, kindness, goodness, faithfulness, gentleness, or self-control? Which one are you?

When you are faced with trying times look first at all that God has done in your life. Remember He loves you. Put Him in your heart and know that nothing of this earth is greater than Him. No pleasure or temptation, no matter how appealing, is worth losing His love.

"For You, O LORD, will bless the righteous; With favor You will surround him as with a shield." (Psalms 5:12 NKJV)

A prayer in times of trouble:

Don't punish me Lord, or even correct me when You are angry. Have pity on me and heal my body. For I am weak without you Lord. My bones tremble with fear, and I am in deep distress. How long will it be? Turn and come to my rescue. Show Your wonderful love and save me Lord. If I die, I cannot praise You or even remember You. My groaning has worn me out. At night my bed and pillow are soaked with tears. And even though sometimes I don't let tears fall, I'm wounded inside. Sorrow has made my eyes dim, and my sight has failed because of my enemies. You Lord, heard my crying, and those hateful people had better leave me alone. You have answered my prayer and my plea for mercy. My enemies will be ashamed and terrified, as they quickly run away in complete disgrace. Amen.

Remember you are surrounded by the shield of God when there seems like nothing but trouble around you. The decision is yours, yet you are not alone.

"For what credit is it if, when you are beaten for your faults, you take it patiently? But when you do good and suffer, if you take it patiently, this is commendable before God." (1 Peter 2:20 NKJV)

You may be tempted to call it quits, but don't. Stay on course. Learn how to control your emotions, thoughts, and what you can't do, call on Jesus. I guarantee you, He can.

Never give up on your recovery. Take it a day at a time. Pray that each day brings you clarity and a clean Spirit.

"But now, thus says the LORD, who created you, O Jacob, And He who formed you, O Israel: Fear not, for I have redeemed you; I have called you by your name; You are Mine." (Isaiah 43:1 NKJV)

Grace is all that God is in the face of all that we're not. Grace is God's gift in a barren place of happiness. Grace can set your worrisome emotions free. Grace is amazing in the face of adversities and can help you triumph over any evil. Be resourceful in finding new ways to get closer to God's grace and keep Him in your heart.

"Set a watch, O Lord, before my mouth; keep the door of my lips." (Psalm 141:3)

Know that God loves you so much today to not let the Devil destroy you. Don't let people, places, or things keep you from God.

Most people don't think that what you say matters. They focus more on other inconsistent issues in their lives. Don't let your words get you into hot water with God. Keep your words clean and clear. Speak His name daily. Praise His name as much as you possibly can to preserve your soul through the strength of your words. And when trouble comes as it possibly will, remember to continue to keep him on your mind and lips, so that trouble looks for an easier target.

Read Romans 12

"Be of good courage, And He shall strengthen your heart, All you who hope in the LORD." (Psalms 31:24 NKJV)

When your faith is tested, your endurance has a chance to grow. Be prepared for all challenges ahead of you.

Read the book of James and ask the Lord for understanding of those words.

"Be strong and of good courage, do not fear nor be afraid of them; for the LORD your God, He is the One who goes with you. He will not leave you nor forsake you."
(Deuteronomy 31:6 NKJV)

A wise open-minded person will gain so much in life. A foolish closed-minded person will lose everything and be in the wilderness going nowhere.

This moment, pledge to be stronger than you've ever been before. Pray that outside influences have no more power over you, ever again. Ask God to strengthen your every step. To heal whatever is left that is unclean in your Spirit and to keep evil from you.

"They shall build houses and inhabit them; They shall plant vineyards and eat their fruit. They shall not build and another inhabit; They shall not plant and another eat; For as the days of a tree, so shall be the days of My people, And My elect shall long enjoy the work of their hands. They shall not labor in vain, Nor bring forth children for trouble; For they shall be the descendants of the blessed of the LORD, And their offspring with them."
(Isaiah 65:21-23 NKJV)

Life is uncertain,
Death is sure,
Sin is the cause,
Christ is the cure.

For example:
Don't wait untill 11pm to repent you may die at 10:30 pm.

Keep God in your heart. Keep progress on your mind. Get through another day without backsliding to your old self.

"For whosoever will save his life shall lose it; and whosoever will lose his life for My sake shall find it."
(Matthew 16:25)

God bless you!

" But the anointing which ye have received of [God] abideth in you, and ye need not that any man teach you: but as the same anointing teacheth you of all things and is truth." (1 John 2:27)

Joy is the echo of God within us, if you have no joy then there's a leak in your spirituality and Christianity. Stay close to God; you will lose the benefits if you don't. Seek His guidance daily. Ask for a greater understanding of His Word.

Joy comes in the morning. You woke up this morning so God has remembered you.

"Be thou strong and very courageous, that thou mayest observe to do according to all the law, which Moses my servant commanded thee: turn not from it to the right hand or the left, that thou mayest prosper whithersoever thou goest." (Joshua 1:7)

Never give up on someone you can't go a day without thinking about. Life is too short. Pray that the Lost be Found. Pray that God is closing all wounds in your life and helping you heal from them. Pray for a quick recovery so that you can spend time, where it is needed, focusing on the Lord.

"He who is slow to anger is better than the mighty, And he who rules his spirit than he who takes a city." (Proverbs 16:32 NKJV)

Forgiveness is not a case of holy amnesia that wipes out the past. Instead, it is the experience of healing that drains the poison from your wounds.

Can you forgive?

If not why?

If you don't forgive your brethren you see daily, how can you expect God (who you cannot see) to forgive you.

"Let all bitterness, wrath, anger, clamor, and evil speaking be put away from you, with all malice. And be kind to one another, tenderhearted, forgiving one another, even as God in Christ forgave you." (Ephesians 4:31-32 NKJV)

To accept being a child of God is to accept the best that God has to offer you. Explore God's will for your life. It's a wonderful journey. It all begins with you and ends with you and ultimately ends with God. God's children are loved. Love can heal all doubt. Doubt can be destroyed by prayer. Prayer changes everything. Everything is good in God's unchanging hands. Seek God like a child seeks early wisdom from mother. Be blessed in all that is His Glory.

Be transformed forever this day. You are not the same person you were when this journey began.

Isn't God good?

"So then, my beloved brethren, let every man be swift to hear, slow to speak, slow to wrath; for the wrath of man does not produce the righteousness of God."
(James 1:19-20 NKJV)

In all, you don't have to be perfect. God uses your imperfections and weaknesses to highlight His grace and mercy toward you. You don't have to be rich. God has all the riches you ever need. You don't have to be powerful. God's word holds all the power you ever really need. All you need is faith, courage, and understanding to begin to get closer to His perfectness, to be a receiver of His riches, and to be a powerful voice of praise for the Lord God Almighty. He alone can get you to that place you so desire to be. He alone can rebuild the broken road you've been traveling and set you on solid ground. He alone can close all wounds.

"But he who endures to the end shall be saved."
(Matthew 24:13 NKJV)

Endure...you are stronger now than you've ever been. Endure...your foundation may shake but will not shatter.
Endure...you learned how action truly speaks louder about your character than words.
Endure...you are on a path to recovery and if your wounds aren't healed believe one day they will be.

Now, Close All Wounds!

> *If you relapse on your own personal recovery with God and you again become wounded, pick up your needle and thread and start all over again.*

If you decide to fall to the wayside, or backslide dust yourself off and start all over again, "GOD said, "I'm, married to the backsliders and I rain on the just and the unjust."

If needed, start over again with the scripture below:

"But seek first the kingdom of God and His righteousness, and all these things shall be added to you."
(Matthew 6:33 NKJV)

 I love you all, Sis Ella Jackson

Bonus Feature

7 MOST POWERFUL PRAYERS

1
A PRAYER FOR HELP

Please listen Lord and answer my prayer! I am poor and helpless. Protect me and save me because you are my GOD. I am your faithful servant and I trust you. Be kind to me! I pray to you all day. Make my heart glad. I serve you and my prayer is sincere. You willingly forgive and your love is always there for those who pray to you. Please listen, LORD, answer my prayer for help. When I am in trouble, I pray, knowing you will listen. No other GODS are like you; only you work miracles. You create each nation to worship and honor you. You perform great wonders because you alone are GOD. Teach me to follow you, and I will obey your truth. Always keep me faithful. With all my heart I thank you. I praise you, LORD GOD. Your love for me is so great that you protected me from death and the grave. Proud and violent enemies, who don't care about you, have ganged up to attack and kill me, but you, LORD GOD are kind and merciful. You do not easily get angry. Your love can always be trusted. I serve you, LORD and I am the child of one of your servants. Look on me with kindness. Make me strong. Save me. Show that you approve of me. Then, my hateful enemies will feel like fools, because you have helped and comforted me. Amen.

2
AN EARLY MORNING PRAYER

I have a lot of enemies LORD. Many fight
against me and say "GOD won't rescue
you!" You are my shield. You give me
victory and great honor. I pray to you and
you answer from your sacred hill. I sleep
and wake refreshed because you LORD
protect me. Ten thousand enemies may
attack me from different sides this day
LORD, but I am not afraid. Come and save
me LORD GOD. Break my enemy's jaws
and shatter their teeth, because you protect
your people. Amen.

3
EVENING PRAYER

You are my GOD and protector. Please
answer my prayers. I was in terrible distress
but you set me free. Now, have pity and
listen as I pray. How long will you people
refuse to respect me? You love foolish
things and you run after what is worthless.
The LORD has chosen everyone who is
faithful to be his very own and He answers
prayers. But, each of you better tremble and
turn form your sins. Silently search your
heart as you lay in bed. Offer the proper
sacrifices and trust the LORD. There are
some who ask, "who will be good to us?"
Let your kindness, LORD, shine brightly on
us. You brought more happiness than a rich
harvest of grain and grapes. I can lay down
and sleep soundly because you LORD will
keep me safe. Amen.

4
A PRAYER IN TIME OF TROUBLE

Don't push me LORD, or even correct me when you are angry! Have pity on me and heal my feeble body. My bones tremble with fear, and I am in deep distress. How long will it be? Turn and come to my rescue. Show your wonderful love and save me LORD. If I die, I can not praise you or even remember you. My groaning has worn me out. At night my bed and pillow are soaked with tears. Sorrow has made my eyes dim, and my sight has failed because of my enemies. You, LORD heard my crying, and those hateful people had better leave me alone. You have answered my prayers and my plea for mercy. My enemies will be ashamed and terrified, as they quickly run away in complete disgrace. Amen.

5
A PRAYER FOR VICTORY

I pray that the LORD will listen when you
are in trouble, and that the GOD of Jacob
will keep you safe. May the LORD send
help from his temple and come to your
rescue from Mount Zion. May he remember
your gifts and be pleased with what you
bring. May GOD do what you want most
and let all go well for you. Then, you will
win VICTORIES, and we will celebrate,
while raising our banners in the name of the
LORD. Amen.

6
THE LORD WORKS MIRACLES

Sing a new song to the LORD! He has
worked miracles, and with His own
powerful arm, He has won the victory. The
LORD has shown nations that He has the
power to save and to bring justice. God has
been FAITHFUL in His LOVE for Israel.
His saving power is seen everywhere on
earth. Tell everyone on this earth to sing
happy songs in praise of the LORD. Make
music for Him on harps. Play beautiful
melodies! Sound the trumpets and horns and
celebrate with joyful songs for our LORD
and KING. Command the ocean to roar with
all its creatures, and the earth to shout with
all His people. Order the rivers to clap their
hands and all the hills to sing together. Let
them worship the LORD! He is coming to
judge everyone on the earth and He will be
honest and fair. Amen.

7
PRAYER FOR PROTECTION

Please listen GOD, and answer my prayer! I feel hopeless, and I cry out to you from a faraway land. Lead me to the Mighty Rock high above me. You are a strong tower where I am safe from my enemies. Let me live with joy forever and find [Protection] under your WINGS, my GOD. You heard my promises and you have blessed me. Just as you bless everyone who worships you. Let the [KING] have a long and healthy life. May he always rule with you, GOD, at your side. May your LOVE and LOYALTY watch over him. Amen

God Loves You.